Early Money

A Guide To Financial Independence For College Students

By: Brandyn Neal

If you enjoy the information in Early Money and find it to be a useful tool getting you started on your financial journey or helping you get back on the right track financially check out my blog www.freedomwealth.org. Freedom Wealth focuses on two topics, entrepreneurship, and personal finance.

Table of Contents

INTRODUCTION

What is important for kids to learn is that no matter how much money they have, earn, win, or inherit, they need to know how to spend it, how to save it, and how to give it to others in need.[1]

— Barbara Coloroso

---

[1] Barbara Coloroso Quotes. (n.d.). BrainyQuote.com.

Preface

My name is Brandyn Neal, and I am a sophomore student at Walsh University in North Canton, Ohio. While I believe that getting a college degree is an incredible accomplishment, I feel that if all you do in your four years as a student is get a degree, then you have let yourself down. Everyone that graduates college gets a degree, but what opportunities will you take to set yourself apart from all of the other students who graduated with you? If your answer is "none," then you have deprived yourself of the most valuable experiences that college can provide for your financial future.

One of my passions is financial literacy. Because of my love and knowledge of the topic, I decided to share this valuable information with all of you. This book uses my unique perspective and position as a college student to show other college-aged readers why getting their finances in order as early as possible is pivotal to reaching financial independence. Achieving a goal of this magnitude is only possible when college students have gained the necessary knowledge to be smart and efficient with their money. The pages of Early Money are littered with the information required to begin down the path of financial literacy and independence.

CHAPTER ONE:

Basics of Money

I believe that through knowledge and discipline, financial peace is possible for all of us.[2]

— Dave Ramsey

• [2] Dave Ramsey Quotes. (n.d.). BrainyQuote.com.

Budgeting

When teaching financial literacy, it is essential to start with budgeting because none of the principles that follow will matter if readers do not know where their money is going. Regardless of how much money you make, if you do not create a plan for your money, then you will never be financially independent. If you do not believe me look at all of the professional athletes, who have made millions of dollars in their careers and then go bankrupt. Every dollar must have a purpose, and the budgeter must understand what that purpose is to one day reach financial independence. As John C. Maxwell said, "A budget is telling your money where to go, instead of wondering where it went."[3] Budgeting is not a glamorous get-rich-quick technique, but that is not what I am here to teach. The art of budgeting is a simple task that is implemented by everyone who is truly serious about becoming financially independent; it will make all the difference in understanding your finances. At the beginning of every month, a financially responsible individual will sit down and make a budget unique to that month. For a monthly budget to be effective, it must be an accurate map of monthly expenses compared to monthly income.

First, a budget must consider all streams of income that are coming in on a monthly basis. That may include allowances from parents, net salary from a part-time or full-time job, passive income streams (see Chapter Three), income from side businesses, or any other form of revenue that is coming in. Once that is done, begin subtracting all of the monthly expenses from the net monthly income – even if it is an expense as small as a five-dollar monthly charge for a student Apple Music account. Understanding where every dollar is going is a necessity when trying to become financially independent.

Significant expenses that most people automatically think of are car payments, gas for the car, tuition payments, phone bills, and groceries. They

---

[3] Author: John C. Maxwell, Source: quoted by Dave Ramsey in The Total Money Makeover

say in boxing that the punch a fighter does not see is the one that ends the fight; that theory holds true in the game of personal finance, too. The expenses that people fail to account for are the ones that keep them back from financial freedom. To get an accurate budget, every expense both small and large needs to be built into the total monthly expenditures. That includes car insurance, car maintenance, parking on campus, entertainment, eating out, school books and supplies, health care maintenance products, haircuts, cleaning supplies, savings account contributions, retirement account contributions, investments, birthday presents, and any other miscellaneous expenses that may be incurred.

Budgeting is just as much about knowing where money is going as it is about understanding spending habits. Personal finance success is only 20% knowledge; the other 80% is about developing healthy financial habits. We spend small bits of money all the time out of impulse, and if we understand what our unique impulse-spending habits are, then we can avoid them more easily. Personally, my impulse habit purchases are Sonic slushies and shopping. We all believe our willpower to be higher than it indeed is, but I have come to find mine is not very strong, so I fight my purchase habits by entirely avoiding them. I try to avoid driving by Sonic unless I am in a real rush because then I will not have time to stop anyways.

I avoid going to stores "just to look around" because that is a surefire way to spend money on things I do not need. The only reason I step foot in a store is that I need something, and in those cases, I go in, get what I need, and leave without browsing. However, it is impossible to take steps to counteract poor habits if they have not been identified by examining previous monthly expenditures.

A tool that I find to be extremely helpful in evaluating my current financial state is an app called Mint. It is completely free to download and use from the App Store with no in-app purchases. One of the biggest reasons I enjoy this app is because it allows me to view all of my financial information in one place. I have all of the information from my investment accounts, savings account, checking account, and my credit card on one platform, which makes it easy to figure out and keep track of my net-worth. On top of that, the app allows users to put together unique-to-them monthly budgets and provides users with weekly updates along with notifications when they are getting close to pre-set budgeted amounts in individual spending categories. Mint also has many other useful features, including the ability to pull a detailed breakdown of users' monthly credit scores with in-depth recommendations for improving them. Another feature I find to be wildly useful is the ability for users to put all of their bills on this app; the platform will keep track of due dates and even allows users to pay bills through the app.

Taking thirty minutes to sit down and put together a well-thought-out budget at the start of each month will set people well on their way to becoming financially independent individuals. The primary point, though, is not just to develop a monthly budget, but to follow it and whenever possible or necessary, to trim down the money being wasted on unneeded items or services.

Keeping up with no one

American society has become so wrapped up in social media that it has created a terrible phenomenon where everyone feels they have to pretend to be something they are not in order to be accepted. Falling into this trap is one of the quickest and easiest ways to end up drowning in debt and never be able to become financially independent. Gary Vaynerchuk, like others less notable figures, has spoken out about the danger of admiring what other people are posting on social media. He makes the point that a majority of the people posting all of the glamorous things on their social media accounts are putting on a show for the world and are not truly as successful, happy, and fulfilled as they want their friends and followers to believe. Vaynerchuk preaches that to be successful people must stop worrying about what everyone else is doing, just put their heads down, and grind their way through to success. I wholeheartedly agree with him; the key to starting something great is patience.

It is not possible to try and keep up with what other people are doing or have. Everyone's story is different, and these different stories allow for different ways of living. Students who come from affluent households and whose parents pay for tuition and living costs may not have to work and can still afford to go out to dinner whenever they feel like it, buy all the new gear when it first comes out, and go out partying on the weekend. On the other hand, students who come from blue-collar families that cannot afford to pay for their children's' tuition and living costs will not be able to indulge in these same luxuries. Students from blue-collar families may have to get jobs – often working nights and weekends – to pay for their schooling, and they may be unable to go out and do the extra things that students from affluent families do.

If students from blue-collar families decide to try and mimic the lifestyles of wealthier students, their behavior would undoubtedly end in disaster. For a short period, they may be able to keep up the act of being a "baller" with the help of credit cards and loans. Sadly, the "baller" life will come to an end because credit card payments will come due and loans must be repaid. When this happens, these students will be left in a heap of high-interest debt and no chance at financial independence.

A saying that I heard a while back that has impacted my life and should impact the lives of other students – if they live by it – is: "Don't compare your step three to someone else's step twenty." That is huge; at some point, all high school and college kids romanticize about their adult careers and making real money. They see older siblings or older friends who have started careers and have begun living adult lives, and they get jealous of the things these siblings or friends have and do. It cannot be emphasized enough, though: do not go through the stress of comparing "your step three" to "someone else's step twenty." Enjoy the process of life and gaining financial independence; it is a long journey that cannot be finished without genuinely enjoying the process. There will be unique advantages and disadvantages at every step of the process that can be learned and exploited.

Not only to become financially free but to be happy in life, you must be able to appreciate the things you have for what they are and not look down upon them because they are not as good as what someone else has. Happiness by way of comparing property is a never-ending cycle that only brings misery. For perspective – because life is 100% perspective – someone who has an income of $32,000 is in the top 1% of personal income in the entire world. People need to understand and appreciate how fortunate they are instead of comparing what they have to someone who has more. Suze Orman says it well: "Stop buying things you don't need to impress people you don't even like."[4]

There is nothing wrong with not having the coolest car, the fanciest clothes, or the newest tech. A car's only purpose is to get its owner from point A to point B safely, so if people own cars that can do that, then they should appreciate it and stop worrying about how their cars look. The same thing applies to clothes. They are merely intended to protect human bodies from the elements of nature and keep private parts private. If people's wardrobes are accomplishing this goal, then they should not concern themselves with getting the new Jordans every time a new pair gets released or buying designer clothing for status, and just appreciate how well what they already have serves them. Phones were created to allow people to get a hold of and stay in touch with friends and family who are far away or otherwise unreachable. Assuming they have phones that can make calls and send texts, people have no reason to worry about all of the features each new phone offers. Students need to stop wasting $800 every time a new iPhone comes out and just appreciate the ones already in their pockets, which give them the ability to stay in touch with their loved ones while away at college. J. Cole said it best, "you ain't never gon' be happy till you love yours."[5]

- [4] Suze Orman. (n.d.). AZQuotes.com.

- [5] J. Cole – Love Yourz. (n.d.). genius.com/J-cole-love-yourz-lyrics

Wants vs. Needs

An individual's ability to understand the difference between a want and need will play an enormous role in their ability to reach financial freedom. Most people understand the general definition of a "need" to be something they must have to survive as human beings, and the definition of a "want" to be something they would like to have, but if they do not get it, will not be detrimental to their well-being. While the majority of the population understands the two terms, they fail to apply these definitions when it comes to making purchases. Consumers tend to be very good at rationalizing "wants" as "needs" to justify their purchases.

Fortunately – or unfortunately, if the reader is someone who categorizes everything as a need – people do not have many necessities for living genuinely human lives. As human beings, we require a roof over our heads, food and water to eat and drink, clothes to put on our backs, and social interaction. In today's first-world society, we can add a few more things to the list of needs if we include phones and some form of transportation. Due to the evolution of technology, our lives are no longer as centralized; we tend to work farther away from home than in generations past and our families are not as centralized in singular neighborhoods in the same way they were in the past. For those two reasons, we can make a reasonable case that transportation and phones are now necessities; however, just because these can be categorized as "needs" does not mean that people should go out and buy the newest and best phone or car. That mindset again becomes a case of "want" instead of "need."

Occasional indulgence can be beneficial, but we must be able to recognize the consequences of neglecting long-term visions and goals for instant gratification. The best way to determine whether a purchase is worth it or not is to consciously ask, "What has to be sacrificed in the future to have this now?" before each purchase. Practicing this method will help cut out those impulse purchases that add up over time because it forces people to think before they spend their money. Another technique I have found to work is to quantify purchases by how many hours of work it will take to afford that purchase. It is a rather good deterrent from going out and wasting money on unnecessary things when people realize that it takes ten hours of work to amass enough money to buy what they do not need. As a college student myself, I understand the "want" to go out and have fun, and all I am saying is to do it intelligently and responsibly.

Luckily for our budgets, we have many options for social interaction that cost no money. When a friend asks to go out for dinner instead of going to the dining hall, ask yourself, "Is this dinner worth putting off saving a down payment on a first home after college?" When a school meal plan has already been paid for, and when students can enjoy the company of the same people on campus, it does not make much sense to eat out all the time. Undoubtedly, at some point in a college career, a person's best friend will want to go out for the third weekend in a row. At that point, the student will have to ask, "Is this night out worth prolonging the time I am going to have to pay interest on student loans?" Sometimes, the answer will be "Yes" – this is college, after all, and we are supposed to have fun and try new things – but even if students turn down one out of every four times they are asked to do something, they will make a huge difference in their finances. I know this is not the most fun way to look at going out and doing things with friends, but it is the responsible way, and it will make life after college significantly more fun. Being responsible with their money now will help keep students out of debt and improve their ability to afford the things they want to have and do as adults.

CHAPTER TWO:

Maximizing What You Have

The waste of plenty is the resource of scarcity.[6]

— Thomas Love Peacock

- [6] Thomas Love Peacock Quotes. (n.d.). BrainyQuote.com.

Free Is for Me

One of the best ways to work around having a shoestring budget is to take advantage of all the free things people love to give to college students. On almost any given night, some organization holds an event on campus that offers students free food just for showing up. If students do not get enough to eat in the dining hall that night, then they can go to an event and get free food; this is a far better option than wasting money on fast food. And who knows? They might even find out they like the organization and want to join it.

College is a tough economic time for a lot of students; make sure you take advantage of giveaways. Many times, for little to no work on the part of students, universities give away free supplies, books, gift cards, and other small prizes.

At Walsh, the Career Center has "T-shirt Tuesday," where a shirt is given out to a student who retweets the Career Center's tweet for that day. Friday mornings, free doughnuts are available to students in the Student Center. Also, Walsh Campus Ministry has a social every Sunday night after mass where free food and a chance to socialize are provided. Those are a few quick examples of campus organizations providing free resources, which can be more beneficial than many students realize for making ends meet while in college.

When college students are short on money, they must leverage their time and efforts to find the things they need in other ways. There are many organizations and businesses on campus and in the community that offer a wide range of free services to students; do not let their generosity go unutilized. At no other point in your life will people be so willing and eager to help you succeed; professionals love to mentor college kids and put them on the right path.

Included
296,614 items
in our
collection

What Is Included

This section is all about getting readers to realize the resources available to them and utilize these resources to the fullest extent. When operating on a tight budget, it does not make sense to pay for services that have already been paid for with school tuition.

One of the most significant ways people fail to take advantage of what is included – I touched on this earlier – is eating out when they have already paid for a meal plan at school. A meal plan generally costs between $3,000 and $4,000 a year, so when taking into account how much students are already paying for food on campus, it is hard to justify going out to eat all the time and spending anywhere from $5 to $20 a trip. If, for some reason, students are forced to miss the dining hall hours, they should consider cooking their meals, a much cheaper solution than eating out. On top of being less expensive than eating out, cooking can be a fun activity that brings friends closer together.

Another expense that is built into college tuition cost is gym access. I understand that the current trend is to be a member of and workout at off-campus gyms, such as Planet Fitness, but students can save $10 monthly, plus the cost of gas and travel time to and from an off-campus gym. It just does not make sense not to use the on-campus gym that students already pay for.

One resource that many students may not know is available to them is tutoring. Many universities offer a certain number of hours per class per week of free tutoring help. Some schools provide professional tutors, while others have peer-tutors - students who have excelled in the areas they tutor in - while yet others offer a mix of peer and professional tutors. The best thing about having peer-tutors available is that they have already taken the course you need help in. Having professional tutors as a resource means, you get the benefit of their experience and familiarity with faculty. Save your money and take advantage of the school-provided tutors.

Students cannot always avoid getting sick or control their allergies, but what they can avoid is paying for the medicine that helps them feel better. Many universities have nurse's offices on campus that are more than willing to supply students with cold and allergy medicine. By going to the nurse's office for over-the-counter medications, students can easily save anywhere from $20 to $100 a year! (Disclaimer: A school nurse is not a replacement for going to your doctor if you need medical attention)

I am not telling anyone to base their college decision on laundry, but Walsh offers free washers and dryers in all of its dorms. That may not seem like much, but things like that will save students a few hundred dollars a year, and incoming students have to consider such things if they know that they are going to be working with a small budget throughout college. When looking to maximize resources as a college student, it is vital to utilize everything that comes along with the yearly cost of tuition.

Fly the Coop

Flying the Coop is a chapter dedicated to not going home on weekends or whenever else there is a chance. Readers are probably thinking, "How can going home to see my family affect my finances?" Well, there are multiple ways that making the trip back home can hinder students' finances in the present and the future. The least obvious – but maybe the most expensive – way going home all of the time hurts students' finances is by stunting their development as young, independent adults. Upon examining the data, college is usually less about the information professors are teaching students and more about putting students in the position to learn necessary life skills – in other words, teaching them how to think. If students are at home with their parents all of the time, they will deprive themselves of the most important things they are paying for with college because they will still have their parents right there to fix all of their problems for them. In turn, they are less likely to do things like laundry, cook, clean, and come up with their own solutions to problems.

A less abstract way going home affects students' finances is the actual monetary cost; unless they live in the area, going home is expensive. Filling up their cars with gas will cost students between $25 and $40, and if they take the toll road home, tolls will cost, on average, $5 to $10 each way. Students who travel home are already spending between $35 and $60 on each trip, and that is before taking into account stopping for a snack on the way or anything they may go out and do with friends while at home.

The previous paragraphs illustrate in actual monetary terms that it is expensive to make the trip home for students who do not live in the area, but that is the least expensive part of going back. The missed opportunity to have a part-time job on the weekend can be very costly, too. If a student has a job that pays a modest $9.00 per hour and works 10 hours each weekend, going home instead of working means leaving around $70 per week, after taxes, on the table. What makes the situation worse is that if students do go home instead of working, they are both leaving money on the table and spending money at the same time.

Most importantly, students who go home on weekends miss all of the networking opportunities that happen during that time. Weekends are when bonds are forged between friends because students are not as busy with school work. In any career, who a person knows and who knows them can be — and likely will be — directly correlated to their lifetime earning power. So, before making that trip home, students should think about all of the ways it will potentially harm their ability to become financially independent. Fly the coop.

Utilizing your Network

Possessing the ability to network consistently and effectively will forever be one of the best things aspiring professionals can do to further their careers. A common misconception is that who a person knows can help them get further in life, but after reading Jeffrey Gitomer's Little Black Book of Connections, I was enlightened – networking is about who knows a person, not just about who a person knows.[7] That is an important distinction because even if you know an influential person, if that connection has no reason to help you, then knowing them does not help you to get ahead in any way.

I would be remiss if I claimed that networking is the way to a successful career and then did not explain

---

- [7] Gitomer, J. H. (2006). Jeffrey Gitomers little black book of connections: 6.5 assets for networking your way to rich relationships. Austin: Bard Press.

what the art of networking is. The literal definition of networking is "the exchange of information or services among individuals, groups, or institutions; specifically: the cultivation of productive relationships for employment or business."[8] However, approaching networking with the mindset of developing contacts so they can help you along the path to success will not bring the desired results. Unquestionably, the most crucial part of networking is always making sure first to add value for potential connections because by operating in this fashion, connections know your intent is not just to take advantage of what they can do to further someone else's career, thus making them more inclined to help you when asked.

Networking is often thought of as going to official networking events were everyone feels uncomfortable and awkward, making the event relatively pointless because the connections are disingenuous and forced. Fortunately, networking does not have to be that way. Opportunities to make connections and network are always around. This mindset must be adopted; it will make all the difference between success and failure. I cannot fathom how many potentially useful connections I have made just by talking to random individuals while waiting in line for ice cream.

- [8] Networking. (n.d.). Retrieved October 15, 2017, from https://www.merriam-webster.com/dictionary/networking

Take advantage of being in the same place as strangers; when at the doctor's office sitting in the waiting room and someone else is waiting, too, take the opportunity to strike up a conversation. When in between sets at the gym, make it a priority to have a conversation with someone new every time. Think about how easy it is to do this: all of these scenarios have a built-in conversation starter because both parties are partaking in the same activity. Take advantage of it.

At work, get to know co-workers on a more personal level than the generic conversations of "Good morning. How are you?" or "Have a good night. See you tomorrow." Find out where they went to school, if they have any kids, what sports teams are their favorites, or what they like to do outside of the office. All of these questions aimed at finding common ground on which to begin building a relationship.

The art of networking does not stop with the initial contact; connections need to see genuine care and interaction to create a level of trust that promotes the continual strengthening of the relationship between two people. A critically important part of networking is the ability to remember things that connections have shared in the past. Even if remembering details is a difficult task, that is okay; instead of seeing it as a hindrance, just take notes! Nothing will make people want to connect with and help you more than when you remember the little things about them. Make it personal when meeting people for the first time; always repeat their names back to them, and if that is not enough for you to remember, write them down. "Good morning Sam" naturally sparks more of a reaction than just saying "Good morning" because now it is a personalized address. If someone shares a big life-event, make a note to remember it and ask how it went the next time you talk to that person. Things like this show people that you have taken a sincere interest in them and make them feel special. Think about previous experiences with people who personalized your conversations and made you feel like they cared about what was going on in your life. Then think about having a conversation with people who could care less about what you had to say and were continually cutting you off to talk about themselves. Which one of these groups was more enjoyable to be around, and which would you be more willing to go out of the way to help? Be the person you would want to help.

Networking can also be pivotal in finding jobs; who people know and who knows them usually will not secure a position, but it can at least get applicants in the door for an interview. From there it is up to them to knock it out of the park and show interviewers not only why they deserve the job, but why the companies have no other option but to give them the positions they seek.

An excellent platform for developing professional connections is LinkedIn. It is the Facebook of the professional world; create a profile of professional information including work history, community involvement, and skill sets. For LinkedIn to be an effective platform for career development, users must be sure to keep their profile professional; users' profile pictures should be of them in professional business attire, and they should limit their posts for the most part to significant accomplishments and inquiries about possible opportunities either for them or their connections.

LinkedIn is such a useful tool for networking because everyone on the platform is there to make new connections and enhance their professional lives. That removes the awkwardness of asking a relative or complete stranger for a favor because everyone on LinkedIn is there to do just that. With that being said, users have to be active to get the full benefits.

Whenever first making a connection on LinkedIn, send an introductory private message introducing yourself, explain the reason for connecting, and state how the connection can be mutually beneficial. The key to this is that the introduction should outline how building a relationship can help add value to your new contact in some way. Providing value upfront will always make people more willing to help you later on when it counts. Shaping your mind always to add value for people will revolutionize the way you live.

CHAPTER THREE:

Creating Passive Income

The moment you make passive income and portfolio income a part of your life, your life will change. Those words will become flesh.[9]

– Robert Kiyosaki

---

[9] Robert Kiyosaki. (n.d.). AZQuotes.com.

Image courtesy of [olovedog] at FreeDigitalPhotos.net

Stop Trading Time for Money

This is the most important thing to becoming financially independent. If people can be making money while they are sleeping, on vacation, in class, at practice, or whatever they may be doing besides working, then their path to financial independence will be much easier than those who are always trading time for money because there are only so many hours to be worked in a day. Making $100,000 a year requires making $11.42 per hour if a person can create a passive income stream that is continually generating revenue 24 hours a day. Breaking it down to a number as small as $11.42 per hour is a much more manageable number compared to only looking at the final sum of $100,000. With the budding of the internet, creating passive income has become possible for anyone who has a Wi-Fi connection and a desire to improve financially.

One way to create a passive income stream is affiliate marketing. Affiliate marketing is when individuals promote another company's products, and that company then pays affiliate marketers a percentage of the sales for bringing in customers. People can do affiliate marketing across many different platforms, such as personal web pages, in blogs or during podcasts. However, marketers promote their affiliates, they must be able to reach a high volume of people to make it profitable beyond just a few dollars a month. Marketing products that you have used and believe in will make your marketing far more impactful for viewers. Even if they promote products they trust and have the best marketing channels available for affiliate marketing, it will not matter if their viewers are not using their link when purchasing an advertised product. The link must be easily assessable for viewers so that they use it when buying the product, or else the selling company will not pay out a commission.

Another great way to make passive income is through blogging. Creating a successful blog requires developing a following – check out my blog freedomwealth.org – that wants to hear about what you have to say as a writer. That can be done by being an authority on the topic that you write about and then marketing the blog to the right demographic to gain popularity. I know that sounds like a lot of work, but it does not have to be. Start by picking a topic that is a passion of yours and write on that daily. Many bloggers will find that it does not feel like work at all. They will also be more successful at growing an audience because their readers will be able to tell that they truly care about the topic. If building a following proves to be too complicated, it is possible to get content writing positions with an established company; this provides you with a built-in viewership. A nice feature of blogging is that the writing style does not have to be as formal as many other forms of writing, making it easier to produce content.

My preferred method of creating passive income is using dividend stock payments as an income stream. For this technique to be as effective as possible, it is necessary to begin as young as possible. Dividend investors will not reap any of the benefits until later in life because they will be reinvesting all of their dividend payments to accumulate shares until retirement. Being a dividend investor who reinvests all dividends is a little bit like being a kid with parents who put presents under the tree three weeks before Christmas, but still has to wait until Christmas to open them. Companies will be paying dividends many years before retirement, but investors will have to wait until they retire to "open" them; however, just like with the presents, I promise it is worth the wait. Assuming the portfolio is built correctly (see Chapter Four), dividend income can be an enormous portion of someone's retirement income.

Creating a podcast or video series ("vlogs") can be a great option for passive income, too. The most important part of podcasting and vlogging is getting and keeping the audience's attention. Two people can be covering the same topic on their shows, but the person who relates it better to the audience will get more viewers, and that is why this is best for high-energy, outgoing people. Once a following has been developed to generate income from their shows, podcasters and vloggers alike can sell ad time to businesses.

I want to make it abundantly clear that creating a podcast or vlog is not as easy as I just made it out to be. But it definitely can be done; a good friend of mine, Jordan Mckelley, started his podcast, called *Run The Globe*, while getting his master's in business administration and serving as a cross country graduate assistant. There are a lot of details for potential podcasters and vloggers to consider, such as perfecting their speech, their presence, and their projection to their audiences; getting the right camera and microphone; and optimizing the lighting for a vlog, along with many other details of creating content. When starting out with little to no money, I would suggest becoming masterful with your cell phone because it is possible to produce both a quality podcast and a video series with just a phone. At the end of the day, though, if a person does not have the charisma and energy to keep an audience's attention, the details will not matter.

An online learning course can also be a great way to create passive income. Individuals who feel like they have valuable information that people would pay to get should not just give it away for free. They can develop and sell an e-course online to create a passive income stream. Successfully creating an e-course requires not only knowing about a particular topic, but also the ability to translate that knowledge in a way that is easily understandable even without being there in person to explain what is meant.

Following the creation of the course, e-course creators must understand their target audience and how to reach that demographic. Depending on what demographic they are attempting to reach, their market penetration strategies will be different, and the best approach will have to be determined through market research. Once their courses have been created, and their target demographics and market penetration strategies have been established, e-course creators collect the residual income every time someone buys their courses. Obviously, follow up courses are not required, but if the first course is successful and sells enough to make continuing the course worthwhile, then creating courses moving forward will be much easier because the basic structure has already been established.

For creative people, selling stock photos, beats, and designs on websites like Fivver can be a great way to make residual income on work they do just one time. It is an even more ideal opportunity if they already love to go out and take photos of unique places and beautiful backdrops, create new beats, or design original digital artwork because now they are getting paid to do something they would do regardless of whether there was money involved or not. Individuals and businesses are continually looking for unique work and will gladly pay a small fee to use the unique things other people create.

Passive income can be obtained in a variety of different ways with the way the world works today. Computer savvy individuals can code an app or design software to generate passive income. If their creations become successful, monetizing an app can be done by allowing companies to put pop-up advertisements on them or charging customers a fee to download the applications. With software that is useful and solves a consumer problem, developers can use either a one-time purchase model or a subscription model that forces customers to pay for the software continually. Once developers have chosen the way they will sell the software, they then have to market it to their intended consumers in a way that demonstrates the software's usefulness so that customers are aware it exists and, therefore, are able and willing to purchase it.

To quantify how lucrative a top-performing app can be, Candy Crush at one point was making $850,000 each day. Now understand, that is an anomaly, but the average app in the Apple Store generates $3,693 each month. That adds up to $44,316 a year, and a sum that large can go a long way towards becoming financially independent.

The last way to generate passive income that I will cover – but certainly not the final possible way – is writing a book. Some people have a passion for writing or just happen to be good at it; why not get paid to do it? Whether they have knowledge that they are dying to share with others or a great fiction adventure to take readers on, there will always be a market for authors who produce well-written books.

To the benefit of authors, it has become significantly more accessible in recent years to self-publish a book, thanks to Amazon. Amazon has two payment structures, depending on the content of the book: either a 35% or 70% royalty. Authors retain complete ownership of their content when they publish through Amazon. Thankfully, authors no longer have to get approval and then come to terms on a deal from a major publishing house, making it possible for anyone to become a published author. While the restrictions are no longer as stringent as they once were, I still encourage self-published authors to find a friend to help them keep to their deadlines and hire a respectable editor to ensure the quality of the book's content and grammar. If authors do those things, they should have no problem creating a great book, even without the help of a publishing house.

Starting a Business

Many students do not realize that there is no better time to start a business than in college. First, students are already in debt and have very few, if any, assets to their name, so they do not have much to lose in the case that the business does not work out. Second, a college campus is a perfect test market for many products or services because there are people from all over the world of varying ages and interests in one centralized place. Third, as I mentioned before, people love to help college students succeed; there will never be as many people willing to help you succeed for free again at any point in your life.

Additionally, schools across the nation have on-campus business incubators dedicated to helping students get businesses off the ground. I am a leader of the incubator on Walsh University's campus; our official name is "The Garage." We are a group of individuals committed to bringing an entrepreneurial presence to campus and helping our student entrepreneurs develop their business ideas from the ground up. The assistance we offer includes teaching our peers basic business principles, developing business plans, creating a minimum viable product, and just providing a space for working in with people to bounce ideas off of. The Garage also makes monetary contributions to help our student entrepreneurs' businesses succeed when we feel they have viable companies and we have the resources available to do so. Everything we do is for students, by students. If interested in learning more about The Garage and the opportunities on-campus incubators across the country can provide for students, take a look at our website: www.walshgarage.com.

SCORE mentoring is also a great free resource for individuals attempting to start a business and looking for professional guidance. Over 300 chapters of the organization exist nationwide, making it an accessible resource for many entrepreneurs. As an organization, SCORE offers similar services to what we do at The Garage, but it has a vast amount of additional resources and connections at its disposal. I used a SCORE mentor when I was in the planning stages of starting my first business. An aspect that separates SCORE from other organizations in its field is that all of its mentors are business professionals who have years of experience in a variety of different areas. If SCORE sounds like a resource that could be of use or if you are just interested in learning more about what they do, more information can be found at: www.score.org.

To start a successful business, entrepreneurs do best when they go into areas that they are not only competent in but also passionate about. Getting a new business off the ground is no walk in the park; there will be many days when an entrepreneur will want to give up on their idea because they have been putting in so much time and effort but are only seeing minimal – if any – results.

Those days are okay; I would even argue they are necessary. Getting through tough days like those is what separates purebred entrepreneurs from the wannabees. They show who is passionate about what they are trying to build, and who got into entrepreneurship because it has become the cool thing to do in today's society, or just want to make a lot of money. Most businesses go a few years before they become truly profitable, so if people start businesses solely to get rich quick, they likely will not be committed long enough to see their companies produce any significant amount of money.

That being said, if entrepreneurs take the time to build businesses with strong principals and high integrity from the very beginning, these can be extremely rewarding and profitable ventures which ideally will be able to one day support their founders. Owning a business is certainly not for everyone; it will be stressful, time-consuming and occasionally will not seem worth it. But being a self-employed business owner is a strong proposition for individuals who do not like answering to bosses, who enjoy flexible work hours, and who desire to leave behind a legacy. No entrepreneur knows for sure if owning a business is the right thing to do until they give it the old college try. For individuals who find out that being business owners is what they were born to do, there will be no better feeling in the world than waking up every morning and going to work for themselves.

CHAPTER FOUR:

Preparing for the Future

By failing to prepare, you are preparing to fail.[10]

— Benjamin Franklin

- [10] Benjamin Franklin Quotes. (n.d.). BrainyQuote.com.

Goal Setting

"Goals allow you to control the direction of change in your favor," according to Brian Tracy.[11] Unless people set clear goals for where they want to be in the next month, six months, ten years, or however long it may be, they have no path to follow and will fall short of their dreams and aspirations every time. Setting a goal is where the process begins, but that in itself is not enough to be successful. Once a target has been determined, the next step is to create an action plan and execute it.

Creating an action plan can be as simple as the task sounds: grabbing a pen and paper then writing down in great detail how to go about reaching the goal from start to finish – including every incremental step in-between. The hard part of the process comes when attempting to put the action plan into effect.

---

[11] Brian Tracy Quotes. (n.d.). BrainyQuote.com.

Sometimes following the plan may require sacrificing in the present. Which may seem like the end of the world, but with a clear understanding of the end goal and what the sacrifices are being made for, it becomes exponentially more doable.

Setting personal finance goals is no different from setting goals for anything else; some goals need to be set in places that seem unattainable. It is okay to fall short of accomplishing a goal that genuinely seems unattainable when setting it because it will still encourage you to strive much harder than if you set goals that are not challenging. With that being said, it is also important to set goals that are achievable because there is something to be said for the special feeling people get when they have worked hard and finally accomplish the goals they set for themselves. Once a goal has been achieved, celebrate it; that is something to be proud of! Taking time to celebrate accomplishments will keep the ambition of wanting to reach your goals alive.

Saving

Everything that I have covered in Early Money up to this point has been with the intent of making sure that there is always money to be saved. The most foolproof way of ensuring continued savings is always to pay yourself first. Savers can accomplish this in many different ways. One option is to take however much money is made in the first half of the first day of the work week and pay yourself with it. For example, if a person works a nine-to-five, Monday-through-Friday job, then everything made from nine to one on Monday goes directly into savings.

I strongly recommend that people always automate their savings; if they are set up to have a certain percentage of every paycheck put in their savings accounts automatically, then they will not have to fight their impulses and make it into a conscious decision to save a part of every paycheck. Doing this, savers will never get used to spending 100% of their paychecks, and because of that, they will have no problem living on 75% to 80% of their total income. Always spending less than the net household income is a major key to becoming financially independent.

In fact, there are multiple places that those who want to be financially independent need to automate their money to go to before ever having an opportunity to spend it. At our age, the first place we need to put money is our unexpected expense accounts. This account is what allows us to sleep easy at night. Having somewhere between $500 and $1,000 set aside in an account for things that could not have been foreseen is a freeing feeling. Once this account is funded, if your car breaks down or your computer decides to die in the middle of finals week, you will have the financial ability to avoid the crises of possibly losing your job for missing work or failing finals because all of your study materials are on a dead computer.

After contributing to an unexpected expense fund account, students should start funding a retirement account. I know what you are thinking: "I am still in college and haven't even started my career yet. Why should I begin saving for retirement?" the reason to start funding a retirement account as soon as possible is that the sooner you start, the easier it is to reach your financial goals and live comfortably after your working days are over. Relying solely on Social Security to fund a retirement can turn what are supposed to be the golden years of your life into the toughest, most stressful years on this earth.

Social Security can be an outstanding piece of a retirement nest egg but is only designed to replace about 40% of people's working incomes. While 40% does not sound so bad, it is estimated that on average people still require 70% of their working incomes in retirement. People must begin planning as early as possible to produce that other 30% comfortably.

The next account that students need to funnel money into automatically is an investment brokerage account. It is imperative to start investing early so that your money can begin working for you instead of you always working for your money. The figure below is an illustration of the importance of getting your money working.

If a student invests $50 each month for the four years spent in college, then the investment totals $2,400; but assuming an average market return of 8% annually, that student will have amassed over $2,900. That is over $500 of money for which the student did not have to work for. Investing in a brokerage account can be a great way to reach short-term money goals – goals besides retirement, like going on spring break with friends senior year.

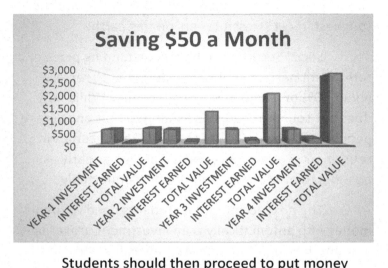

Students should then proceed to put money into a large purchase fund. This fund is not to be touched until they decide to do something such as start a business, put a down payment on a house, or purchase a new car. This fund is created specifically for those types of purchases and will help avoid taking on debt and paying high interest rates. With money stored away, they will also be able to get lower mortgage rates and avoid paying mortgage insurance, which can raise monthly bills by hundreds of dollars until a 20% down payment amount is reached.

Having money in a fund like this can even make it possible to purchase a car with no loan at all. Paying cash for a vehicle cuts out having to pay any interest on the purchase. That is beneficial because cars are depreciating assets, so if it is possible to avoid making continual payments on something that is losing value, doing so is considered a huge advantage. An added perk of owning vehicles outright is that owners can take out equity loans against their cars if they get in a tight spot and need to. Having money stored away in a large purchase fund also gives aspiring entrepreneurs the flexibility to start and operate their businesses without requiring an immediate profit.

Finally, students should begin contributing to an emergency fund. As the name implies, withdraws are only to be made from this account in case of a severe emergency. Wanting pizza at two in the morning after a long night out does not constitute an emergency – though sometimes it feels like it should. Usually, an emergency fund would be the first account to be funded, but because we are college students, the order is a little different. An emergency fund is not as important to us as it is to those who are already out in the workforce because we have fewer financial responsibilities – in fact, many of us do not yet have any – to cover in the case that we were to lose our jobs.

No standard dollar amount can be given for the perfect emergency fund, but the general rule is three to six months of living expenses. This amount supplies us with a cushion to fall back on should something happen, and we no longer have any money flowing in. If these rules of savings are followed, they will put anyone in a strong financial position for the future.

Investing

Investing comes in many different forms and strategies; it is each person's duty to find which ones work best for their situation and to utilize those strategies on the path to reaching financial independence. Investment strategies will differ depending on what the investing goal is; retirement accounts are handled in a vastly different fashion than a general brokerage account, and I will go over why in the following pages. Forms of retirement accounts include 401(k)s, Roth 401(k)s, Individual Retirement Accounts (IRAs), and Roth IRAs.

401(k)s are employer-sponsored accounts that employees contribute to with pre-tax income, then pay tax when they begin to make withdrawals in retirement. Generally, employers will offer a dollar for dollar match of however much employees contribute to the account up to a certain percentage of their annual salaries. Essentially, this is free money to employees, and it should always be the first retirement account contributed to, at least until reaching the full employer match.

The maximum contribution limit as of 2017 for people under fifty is $18,000 per year of pre-tax income, not including the amount matched by employers. Unlike other authorities in the past, I do not feel maxing out 401(k) contributions is necessarily the best option to prepare for retirement because in recent years research has shown that many 401(K) plans are limited in their investment options and charge exceptionally high fees. Roth 401(k)s have the same basic rules as regular 401(k)s except that they are funded with after-tax money; therefore, withdrawals are tax-free at the age of 59 1/2. Unfortunately, 401(k)s are generally only offered to full-time employees, so individuals who work part-time will likely be unable to take advantage of the free money being provided.

If ineligible for a 401(k), the next option to save for retirement is an IRA, a Roth IRA or both. Thankfully, no employer is needed to open either type of IRA. Opening an IRA is as simple as opening an account with one of the abundant brokerage firms available today. Before opening an account, make sure you do your homework on all of the fees that each firm charges. Many companies have minimums to open an account as well as different annual fees and trading cost structures.

The brokerage firm I found to have the best overall fee structure was Fidelity, which has no minimum to open an IRA and no annual fees to go along with its recently lowered trade commission charges of $4.95 per trade. Benefits do not end there with Fidelity; it also offers new customers ten free trades for opening an account with its mobile app, which comes to almost $50 of free money. One issue I encountered when opening an account with Fidelity was the company's old-school approach to customer communication.

At the time, I had just turned eighteen, so Fidelity was unable to verify my identity by my social security number, which would not have been a problem at all if it had not been for their refusal to handle the matter through any form of technology. They left me no option but to drive an hour to the nearest Fidelity location and open my account in person. Aside from that, I have had no problems working with Fidelity, and I find their platform to be very intuitive and great for doing stock research. Each brokerage firm has benefits and drawbacks depending on how much money an investor plans to invest, trade frequency, and investment types; it is up to individual investors to decide which brokerage firm suits them best.

Investing Methods

The first method of investing I am going to cover is the "buy and hold forever" method; this method has been made famous by one of my idols – the Oracle of Omaha, Warren Buffet. This strategy can best be utilized in a post-tax retirement account (Roth 401(k) or Roth IRA) since the time horizon is the longest and the tax advantages allow investors to avoid the headaches that would arise in a non-tax advantaged account due to the payment and reinvestment of dividends. What I mean by "headaches" is that not only would investors be taxed on every dividend payment they received for holding the stock through the years, even though they are not receiving the dividend as cash, but investors would also have to log all of the shares purchased with dividends and the cost per share for each of those purchases in order to avoid being double-taxed on all of their dividend distributions. Double taxation on dividends equates to 30% of the total dividend payment.

Buying and holding is made most effective by beginning as early as possible because this gives investors' money and shares the most extended time horizon to work for them. As with any form of investing, to be most successful, investors should stay within what Buffet calls their "circle of competence" and businesses that operate within that circle. Reaping the most exceptional long-term returns from buying and holding requires investors to be shareholders in high-quality companies that pay continuously growing dividends and to reinvest all of those dividends continually until retirement.

Reinvesting dividends is easy to accomplish by setting up a dividend reinvestment plan (DRIP) with a brokerage firm. DRIPing dividend payments offers benefits such as purchasing shares without paying commission and sometimes receiving a small discount in share price. Adding to those benefits, DRIPing automates investing, taking personal emotions out of the equation. Also, the technique averages down the cost-per-share basis, as the dividend can buy more shares when the stock is cheap and fewer shares when the stock is at a high price.

As stated before, it is essential for a successful buy and hold account to be based in high-quality companies that pay healthy dividends and have grown – and will continue to grow – for many years. A useful list called the "Dividend Aristocrats" consists of companies in the S&P 500 which have paid and grown their dividends uninterrupted for at least 25 years.

Unfortunately, once a company has been able to reach this status, its reputation is priced into its share price, often making it overpriced. When a company of this nature goes "on sale" due to turmoil in the business, it is an opportune time to initiate a position. When picking their dividend stocks, investors have to weigh the risks against rewards, as stocks that are not as stable will pay a high dividend yield, while the Aristocrats have an average dividend yield of around 2%.

The best dividend portfolios will include a combination of riskier and safer dividend stocks. In my research, I found a methodology by a writer on the website Seeking Alpha who goes by the name of Dividend House.[12] Her methodology is exactly what her name says: building a dividend portfolio using the same process used to construct a home. The method reflects five different sections of a home. The largest and most important part of the collection is the core stocks; they are the "foundation" of the house and make up at least 50% of the portfolio's income. Core stocks consist of well-established dividend-paying stocks, such as the Dividend Aristocrats. Only well-established companies can be placed in the foundation of a dividend house because those shares are what

- [12] Dividend House Dividend growth investing, long only. (2015, March 03). The Dividend House DGI Portfolio: The Good, The Bad, And The Ugly. Retrieved October 15, 2017, from https://seekingalpha.com/article/2966946-the-dividend-house-dgi-portfolio-the-good-the-bad-and-the-ugly.

hold up the rest of the house regardless of what the market is doing, so investors have to be able to rely on them in both good and bad times.

After laying the foundation, the next step is to move on to the supporting stocks, or "walls," of the dividend house. These supporting stocks should make up no more than 25% of the total portfolio income. Supporting stocks are still strong dividend payers with at least a short track record of paying and growing dividends, but have not yet shown the level of consistency the core stocks have. Because these stocks are not as highly valued as core stocks, they will likely have slightly higher dividend yields than their Aristocrat counterparts.

After the walls are up, the "roof" can go on the dividend house. According to Dividend House, the auxiliary stocks that make up the roof should produce 15% of the portfolio's total income. I define auxiliary stocks as companies that have either just begun paying a dividend or do not have a healthy dividend coverage. A healthy dividend coverage means that the percentage of a company's earnings per share (EPS) being paid out in dividend payments is less than 60%. That usually means that the company has plenty of retained earnings to increase the dividend amount or to cover it should the profits take a slide.

The final two pieces of the dividend house portfolio are the "bench" and the "garden." Bench stocks consist of stocks that were once in a more vital portion of the house, but have underperformed; that could mean the company has reduced or cut its dividend completely, or it may have just not grown its dividend at an anticipated rate. Due to the fact that they have underperformed expectations, investors should trim these positions and wait for them to turn the proverbial ship around, or they should wait for a good time to exit the stock altogether.

Garden stocks are an utterly speculative play. The garden is made up of stocks that are struggling and have either recently cut their dividends or are likely to reduce them soon. The garden is where investors place stocks that – if their assumptions about the company's future ability to pay a stable dividend are correct – will be profitable, but the chances for this happening are slim. Consequently, garden and bench stock combined should make up only 10% of the total dividend house income.

"Growth stock investing" is the next method I want to go over. This strategy puts less importance on buying dividend-paying companies and accumulating as many shares as possible. The goal of growth investing is to buy a company for which there is a strong reason to believe that the company's stock will appreciate in share price in a rather significant way. Due to the liquid nature of this type of investing, it lends itself well to a regular brokerage account because there are no restrictions on withdrawing money out of the account.

The type of investors who will use this strategy most successfully are those who are attuned to everything that is going on in the world around them. Investors who have the ability to notice early on that a product or service is becoming popular or trending can take advantage of this gift, and invest in the industry before the price of stocks begins to reflect its popularity and trendiness.

One of my favorite places to look for possible growth stock plays is among the daily market's biggest losers. Here, investors can occasionally find quality companies that have hit hard times and are at or near 52-week lows in stock price. When a company that has been around for a long time and has a strong reputation sits at a 52-week low, it can be an awesome opportunity for a growth play if the core fundamentals of the business have not changed.

Implementing this strategy, successfully, requires investors to be cognizant of and smart about their trading. When buying and selling stocks, investors have to remember that trading commission will eat a portion of the profits – as will the tax on any gains. One way to avoid commission fees, if investors are using a method other than buy and hold, is to open a brokerage account with a platform called Robinhood, which has $0 trading fees.

The reason this does not work with a buy and hold approach is that Robinhood does not offer Roth IRAs and it does not allow users to reinvest dividends directly. To keep even more of the gains, savvy investors can lower their tax rates by holding investments for at least a year and one day. Doing this will trigger the long-term gains tax rate. Depending on the tax bracket, long-term gains tax is between zero and twenty percent; comparatively, short-term gains are taxed at rates between fifteen and thirty-five percent.

For a majority of individuals, the best method of investing will be through "index funds" and "exchange trade funds" (ETFs). This form of investing allows investors to reach diversification easier by getting exposure to entire sectors of the markets instead of trying to pick one winning stock. For example, if investors want to invest in the energy sector because they think it is getting ready to take off, instead of investing only in one company, like General Electric, they can purchase an index fund or ETF that holds all of the major companies in the energy sector. Doing so ensures that if the industry appreciates, they are positioned to share in the profits.

Indexing is the best option for the average investor who does not have the time or knowledge to do extensive research on multiple individual stocks. One of the most important factors when choosing an index fund is making sure that the fees are low, or else they will erode any profits that might be made, but this is not the only factor to consider. Investors should also look at what kind of companies are in the portfolio, the Beta (risk level relative to the overall market) of the fund, and the weight (percentage of the total portfolio) of each stock in the portfolio.

An option I use for diversification is the app Acorns; it is a robo-investing app that allows users to decide how aggressive they want to be and then allocates their money accordingly. The platform uses the aforementioned ETFs strategy to diversify holdings into many different companies and sectors. Since I have been using this app, I have seen close to a 7% annual return on my investment; this performance is modest, but it is still a better return than what bonds would provide. Acorns also simplifies the investing process for its users. Acorns offers a multitude of features that make it easy for students to begin investing. First, if students sign up with their school email, Acorns does not charge any fees. Second, users can make investments as small as five dollars. Third, users can also set roundups on their debit card purchases, which rounds up all of their transactions to the nearest whole dollar and makes them invest every time they spend money without even realizing it. Because of these features, I use the platform, and I feel it is a great place for all college students to start investing.

Committing

Making a commitment and staying true to that promise long after the mood it was made in has left will be beneficial both during college and throughout life. Once students have decided to take on the massive commitment that is going to college, they must make a series of smaller commitments. To be successful in their college careers, students need to choose their majors and commit to those majors. Next, students have to commit to dedicating themselves to gaining as much knowledge as possible to prepare for their future careers. Partying is undoubtedly a part of the college experience, but if students party too often and fail to take their school work seriously from the start, that will quite possibly be the costliest broken commitment of their lives.

Deciding late in their college careers that the major's students chose as first-year students are no longer the ones they want to pursue can also be a costly broken commitment. Often, this leads to extra years of schooling, which is expensive in two ways.

First, the obvious added tuition cost is likely to be higher than in previous years because most scholarships and grants only cover four-years, meaning students will likely have to pay full price to attend college for an extra year. Second, late changes in majors prolong the amount of time until students can enter the working world, costing them not only their full-time salaries but also valuable working experiences.

Commitments are not limited to big decisions like going to college; they can be much smaller than that. For example, if you decide no longer to go to Starbucks because it is overpriced and instead are going to make a pot at home every morning, commit to it. Making that commitment and following through with it will do wonders for your financial health. The chart below displays how much money would be wasted if a person purchased a Grande Latte from Starbucks every day. The cost seems minimal when looking at individual purchases, but when looking at the price holistically, the numbers quickly get large. I am sure there are better things you can do with $1,226 a year than buy coffee; one option I will suggest is investing that money. If people invested the same $1,226 a year from the time they were eighteen until the full retirement age of sixty-three, assuming an average annual return of 8%, they would have an extra $319,576 to spend in their retirements! Is a daily latte worth giving up that kind of money?

Latte	Cost
Day	$ 3.65
Week	$ 25.55
Month	$ 102.20
Year	$ 1,226.40

For financial independence, commitment to a lifetime of saving and investing is required. If people always save first, then they will never face the problem of spending more than they are making; and if they consistently invest their money, then their money will always be working for them.

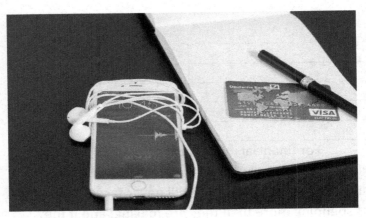

Building Credit

Getting started with building credit can be a daunting, even scary task. How do lenders expect people to improve their credit score when no one will give them a loan – and credit cards seem like financial death traps? First of all, if used properly and intelligently, credit cards can be an excellent way for people to improve their credit scores when they are young. One factor in improving credit scores is a history of paying bills on time, so it can be beneficial for students to open credit cards and then choose a single monthly expense to pay for with them, such as gas. The key to this tactic, though, is that the cards are used responsibly, keeping the usage rate below thirty percent of the total available credit and that the card is paid off in full and on time every month. That ensures that cardholders never pay astronomically high-interest rates on credit cards, which can be as high as twenty-five percent.

Another factor credit bureaus consider is "credit age," which is how long people have had open lines of credit; the older the credit age, the better effect it has on people's credit scores. Having an overall credit age of nine years or longer is considered to be excellent, and will be a substantial positive factor on a credit score. The next time your parents or friends advise against using a credit card, know for these reasons they are misinformed.

Another way to improve a credit score is to rent either a house or apartment, as with credit cards, always pay your bill on time. This method is helpful because renters do not need to take out loans to get installment payments (recurring payments) on their credit. Unfortunately, not all landlords report your payment history to the credit bureaus, so check with your individual landlord to see if they will.

When formulating a score, the credit bureaus do not only consider payment history but examine diverse areas of credit history, and that is why it is essential for people to get both revolving credit and installment payments on their credit. Creditors look at individuals' abilities to hold long-term jobs and to be responsible with the money in their bank accounts when deciding whether or not they are worthy of being approved for loans. Applying for multiple credit cards or loans in a short period is something that many students may not realize can have an adverse effect on their credit scores. When someone applies for a form of credit, the lender makes a hard inquiry that shows up on people's credit scores. When they have multiple inquiries in a short period, lenders infer that they are hurting for money and take this as a bad sign. Using these tips can be a great way to improve a credit score and the likelihood of being able to secure a loan when it is most needed.

Building good credit is so important for young students because credit makes the world function. Governments, large companies, and individual people all use credit to get themselves to where they are and where they want to be. When people have high credit scores, using their credit to prosper is possible because they get low-interest rates and can avoid paying a premium for items bought on credit. Low interest makes it easy to generate returns higher than the cost of capital. If credit is used correctly, it will allow people to advance their lives in ways that would not be possible without it.

CHAPTER FIVE:

Power of Time

Someone is sitting in the shade today because someone planted a tree a long time ago.[13]

— Warren Buffett

• [13] Warren Buffett Quotes. (n.d.). BrainyQuote.com.

Compound Interest

Compound interest is all about getting money to work for you so that you do not have to work for it. Albert Einstein, one of the greatest minds ever to live, once said that the eighth wonder of the world is compound interest. It really can do amazing things when given enough time to work its magic. My dad once said to me, "You're a money guy. If I offered you $40,000 today or I gave you a penny today and told you that every day for the next 30 days that penny will double, which would you take?" That is an obvious choice: "Give me the $40,000 right now!" That would be wrong; at the end of those 30 days, the penny would have compounded to $5,368,709. While it is not realistic to expect to double your principal daily, this example nonetheless shows the power of compound interest.

Impatient people go wrong when they expect compound interest to have a profound effect immediately; it is the most long-term play in the game. Compound interest has its strongest effects at the end of the compounding period because the amount it is compounding on continues to grow with interest payments being paid interest on interest. For example, if an investor makes a $10,000 investment that is set to yield 8% annually, it will produce a nice profit of $800 ($800/$10,000 = 8%) after the first year, but after 40 years, that same 8% yield is now paying $17,379 ($217,245 * .08 = $17,379). That is a 174% return on the initial investment. The $234,624 amassed over those 40 years is a 2,346% return on the initial investment ($234,624/$10,000 = 2,346%), and a return got for doing no work after investing the $10,000 besides watching over the investment to ensure it is still a good one. No other force in the world besides compound interest can create a return of that nature.

One of my favorite types of compound interest is reinvesting dividends. I have covered this in previous chapters, but I want to emphasize DRIPing because of its immense power. Say someone bought ten shares of The Reality Company every year from age eighteen to the full retirement age of sixty-three; at the current trading price of $54.20, it would cost about $550 each year including commission fees. For simplicity, assume the stock price appreciates by 2% annually, and the dividend grows by 5% annually, which is in line with the annual growth since 2014. Under these conditions, this individual would purchase 450 shares of Reality company for a total price of $24,877.80 spread out over forty-five years. That is not the impressive part, though. By reinvesting the dividends monthly for the entire forty-five years, this person will end up with much more than 450 shares. The patience and commitment to investing will be rewarded with 1,556.31 shares of The Realty Company that are worth $84,352. But the best thing about reinvesting dividends is that the added shares are not where profits end. This person now has a position that makes $326.76 each month and $3,921.12 each year in retirement income once DRIPs are turned off, and the investor starts collecting the dividends. That income has no effect on the principle of $84,352. When compound interest is given time to work, incredible things will happen without a lot of effort. (Disclaimer: I am not recommending that anyone open a position in The Reality Company or any other without due diligence.)

Risk Tolerance

Risk tolerance plays a significant role in composing a portfolio, and younger investors can have higher tolerances for risk. When we are in college, our time horizon is so long that our portfolios should consist of almost all – if not all – stocks because we can afford to wait out market fluctuations. Stocks historically yield a much higher percentage than other investment vehicles such as bonds, CDs, or just saving money as cash. As we get older – and our time horizon shortens because retirement approaches – we have to change the allocations of our portfolio.

Another factor of risk tolerance and portfolio allocation is individual personalities. Some people – regardless of their age and how long they have until they need to access their money – cannot handle seeing dips in their account value, and they feel a strong urge to sell to stop the loss. They fail to realize, however, that if they choose high-quality companies, the fluctuations do not matter because they will correct themselves. Investors do not lose anything until they sell their position and lock in that loss.

Contrarian investing and risk tolerance go hand in hand. When a usually beloved company falls on hard times, and all of the investors who fear losing money sell their positions, the stock devalues, and this creates a great buying opportunity for investors who are not scared of a little risk. Now they see a chance to buy blue-chip companies at a discounted price. After purchasing shares at such a cheap valuation, contrarian investors will sit on the stock and ride out the ups and downs, waiting for it to recover its usual prices or possibly even go higher. Contrarian investing is made even more effective when the undervalued company pays a dividend because then investors lock in the higher yield and get price appreciation as well. Opposing the market sentiment will often pay off handsomely; a mentor once told me, "If you agree with the majority, it is time to rethink your opinion."

Knowledge

The most powerful thing anyone can gain with time is knowledge, and often failure is the best teacher. As a society, we have to alter our perspective on failure. Right now, failure is looked at with a sense of finality that does not truly go hand in hand with failure. All failure does is present an opportunity to learn what does not work with the chance to think of a new solution. Once we stop looking at failure as a final destination and start looking at it as a part of the journey to success, our ability to gain knowledge will increase exponentially. There is no better time than college to acquire as much knowledge as possible because it is a time for young adults to try new things without resistance; it is like starting a new business.

While failure is a sizeable part of everyone's journey to acquiring knowledge, there is more to it than failure alone. The most successful people learn from the mistakes of others – and this, too, is a crucial way of acquiring knowledge. To put yourself in the best possible position, read books written by top people in the industry you aspire to be in, to gain the useful insight they have learned through their years. Reading books of this type will help you avoid some of the mistakes along the way because their authors have already lived through those stages of life that their readers are going through; they made their mistakes, and they wrote their books so that their readers do not have to make them, too.

One of the great philosophers of our time, Meek Mill, once said, "If you don't know where you make your mistakes, that's your worst mistake: not knowing where your mistakes are at."[14] Making mistakes is required for success, but you also have to be able to recognize your mistakes and adjust your life to reach success. The moment you stop making mistakes and learning is the moment you will stop being successful.

---

[14] Meek Mill Quotes. (n.d.). BrainyQuote.com.

Testimonials

Wealth is the ability to fully experience life.[15]

-Henry David Thoreau

- [15] Henry David Thoreau Quotes. (n.d.). BrainyQuote.com.

Bill Arfaras

Bill is a junior at Walsh University, and he is well on his way to becoming financially independent. He currently owns a print shop, called 1st Choice Web Solutions, which is based in Youngstown, Ohio. He started the company in the eighth grade because his father was complaining about business cards being so expensive. Bill saw an opportunity to make money, and he ran with it. Through the years, he has expanded the shop from only producing business cards to now producing pamphlets, banners, billboards, screen prints, and embroidery. The key to his financial independence is not that he owns the business, but that he began growing the business and hiring employees so that he could start making money without having to be present in his own time.

As crazy as it may sound, Bill's path to financial independence started long before he opened his printing business in the eighth grade. He is unsure of his exact age then, but he believes it to be somewhere between five and seven when one day he threw away change and his dad, he says, "tore him a new one." That experience made him understand the value of money regardless of how small the amount. He recalls another experience that set him on the right path – a conversation with his grandfather. His grandpa told him always to save a piece of what he makes. After those two experiences, Bill has always been sure to be diligent with his money.

Unfortunately, he says, coming up through the school system he never had any formal financial education. Bill was lucky to receive this knowledge from family members; most kids never do. Evident in his accomplishments thus far in his life, Bill is a smart guy, and he may have been on to something when he told me that schools should intertwine personal finance with the basic math classes that every student has to take.

Bill's is a fantastic story about getting an early start on taking control of his finances. He challenged and defied the thought process that people cannot own businesses and start making real money until they have formalized training and experience. He has proved that – no matter your age – if you are willing to work hard and use the principles in this book, you can get ahead financially. Bill is a good friend of mine, and it brings me joy to see that the same principles discussed in Early Money helped him become so successful.

Brandy Campbell

Brandy does very well for herself and her family as the Sr. Manager, Global Payroll at Fanatics. Incredibly, she recently achieved her goal of completing her master's in business administration before the age of forty with less than a week to spare. Things were not always so good for her; shocking to all who meet her today, she dropped out of high school when she was 16 and had filed for bankruptcy with two kids by the age of 20. Having gotten off to a rocky start in her financial life, she realized that she needed to begin taking the necessary steps to get back on her feet.

Her story of financial rebirth began when she decided to earn her GED and then get her first college degree in an effort to start a career. Along with taking the necessary steps to start a career, she also began remodeling her financial philosophies. Brandy started saving a portion of her paycheck in a 401k account and repaired her credit score through smart, responsible spending.

A strategy Brandy uses to continue growing as a person, and a payroll manager is moving on from a company after she has solved the problems in her department. She takes the new skills she has learned to a new business where she can put them to work on resolving the issues of her new company's payroll department. This strategy proves to be far more lucrative than staying with a single company for her entire career.

After many years of a fierce financial makeover, Brandy has positioned herself to begin her own business. She soon plans to own rental properties to generate another revenue stream on her way to becoming financially independent. Eventually, she plans not only to possess rental properties but also to flip houses. Even though Brandy was able to turn around her financial situation, she stresses the importance for young people not to put themselves behind the proverbial eight-ball the same way she did.

Brandy is my mother, and I could not be prouder of what she has been able to accomplish this far in her career – or be more thankful for all of the opportunities she has afforded me through her hard work.

Scott Glasgow

Scott is the founder of FinMango, a non-profit organization based in North Canton, Ohio. The mission of FinMango is to empower students – both locally and globally – by tearing down barriers to financial literacy through education. He believes that when schools fail to teach even the basics of financial literacy, they do students a great disservice. Because many schools do not teach their students this information, Scott says that financial advisers can take advantage of their adult clients by using complicated terms to confuse them. This unfair practice motivated him to found FinMango and share the gift of financial knowledge with students in Ohio and across the globe – a gift that keeps on giving.

Scott says that an early knowledge of personal finance made him understand "the relationship between time and money," and because of that understanding, he has been a "minimalist" since he can remember. He recognized the importance of starting down the path of financial independence at a young age, utilizing the great effects of compound interest. When given an ample amount of time to work its magic, compound interest is one of the strongest tools for achieving financial independence. Scott passionately described his money cycle as: "make it, save it, grow it, spend it (a little bit) and donate it." Living by that cycle gave him the ability to self-fund FinMango and empower thousands of young people to live financially literate lives.

My only goal for Early money is to set my peers on the right path to reach financial independence. Becoming financially independent provides individuals a unique freedom unattainable in any other way. If you ever have any questions about anything financial or entrepreneurial, please do reach out to me at brandyn@freedomwealth.org!

93131960R00049

Made in the USA
Columbia, SC
06 April 2018